The Alkaline Diet

A 14-Day Alkaline Diet Plan

Over 75 Delicious Alkaline Diet Recipes To Satisfy Every Craving

Tatiana Barbosa

TABLE OF CONTENTS

Introduction

The Alkaline Diet

Alkaline Ash Diet and Alkaline Acid Diet are just two namesakes of this type of diet which focuses on eliminating most of the foods that are acid-forming and focusing on those that are alkaline-forming. The aim is to balance the body chemistry which is the utmost needed requirement to maintain good health, prevent inflammations and help loss weight.

The Science of Food Digestion

When we eat food, they are digested in the stomach using gastric juices and metabolic enzymes from the liver and pancreas, turning them into energy, nutrients, fats, vitamins, minerals, fibres and ashes that are absorbed by the bloodstream and distribute to the different tissues of the body.

The food ash can either be neutral, acidic or alkaline depending largely on the chemical composition of the food source. Most commonly, fruits and vegetables leave alkaline residues while meat and wheat produce acidic ashes.

A healthy human body usually keeps substantial amount of alkaline reserves to combat any imminent overflow of acidity from acid-forming foods and unhealthy lifestyle such as lack of sleep and exercise, stress and presence of sickness. When these reserves are depleted, health can be extremely jeopardized for a correct acid-alkaline ratio is paramount for proper functioning of all the body tissues.

Consequences of an Acidified Body Tissue

Acidified body tissues will become weak.

It is because acidified body cells are deprived of the required energy and oxygen to sustain a healthy immune system. The capacity of the body to repair, replenish or regenerate cells is hampered thus limiting the body's biological and physiological functions.

This will result to many unhealthy body tissue conditions and maladies, such as low-grade and chronic acidosis, bone diseases, arthritis, nutrient deficiencies, muscular weakness and diseases. The list will go as far as heart disease, cancer, strokes, colon disease, and a number of digestive health complications.

The Alkaline Acid Regimen

This diet's main success lies in the proper balancing of food intake. A more alkaline diet is needed to offset the surge of acid-producing factors brought by unhealthy lifestyle, and an array of acid-forming comfort foods.

It is therefore important, first of all, to know what we are eating. Topping the list for alkaline-forming food include spinach, figs and watermelon. While oyster, beef, and walnut lead the list for acid-forming food. A list is provided below for the Acid-alkaline category of most common food we eat.

The second thing to do to start this diet right, is to formulate a meal plan that includes the most and not so alkalizing foods and combining them with low to moderate acid-forming foods. The rule of the thumb is a meal should contain 80 % of the Alkalizing foods while the remaining is allotted for acid –forming foods. This cookbook features a 14-day meal plan that follows this rule of proper food combination. Ingredients in RED colour are the acid-forming foods.

Apart from the meals, there are a lot of refreshingly healthy drinks that can effectively offset the effects of acid-forming foods. From a simple soda water to meticulously prepared green smoothie, these liquids can neutralize a can of beer and even add to the alkaline reserves of the body.

Lastly, make use of the alkalizing power of herbs and spices. They can add power and wonderful twists to an array of dishes. Always garnish with parsley or mint and explore Mediterranean cuisine.

List of Common Alkaline-forming Foods

Highly Alkaline

Broccoli, Sprouts, Grasses, Cucumber, Kale, Kelp, Spinach, Parsley, Sea Vegetables (Kelp), Green drinks Cabbage, Celery, Collard Greens, Avocado, Beetroot, Capsicum/Pepper, Endive, Garlic, Ginger, Green

Beans, White Haricot Beans, Chia, Lettuce, Mustard Greens, Okra, Onion, Radish, Red Onion, Arugula, Tomato, Lemon, Lime, Butter Beans, Watermelon, Chestnut

Moderately High Alkaline

Apple, Apricot, Banana, Blackberry, Blueberry, Cranberry, Grapes, Mango, Mangosteen, Orange, Peach, Papaya, Pineapple, Strawberry, Apple Cider Vinegar, Fresh Fruit Juice, Organic Milk (unpasteurized), Mineral Water, Alkaline Antioxidant Water, Green Tea, Herbal Tea, Kombucha

Mildly Alkaline

Watercress, Grapefruit, Coconut, Artichokes, Cauliflower, Carrot, Chives, Courgette/Zucchini, Leeks, New Baby Potatoes Peas, Asparagus, Brussels Sprouts, Rhubarb, Swede, Buckwheat, Quinoa, Spelt, Lentils, Tofu, Other Beans & Legumes, Goat milk, Almond Milk, Most Herbs and Spices, Avocado Oil, Coconut Oil, Flax Oil/ Udo's Oil,

List of Common Acid-forming Foods

Neutral / Mildly Acidic

Amaranth, Millet, Oats/Oatmeal, Spelt, Black Beans, Chickpeas/Garbanzos, Kidney Beans, Cantaloupe, Currants, Fresh Dates, Nectarine, Plum, Sweet Cherry, Soybeans, Rice/Soy/Hemp Protein, Brazil Nuts, Pecan Nuts, Hazel Nuts, Sunflower Oil, Grape seed Oil, Freshwater Wild Fish, Rice and Soy Milk, Honey, white sugar, raw sugar, yogurt

Moderately Acidic

Wild Rice, Brown Rice, Wholemeal Pasta, Ketchup, Mayonnaise, Butter, Oats, Rye Bread, Wheat, Wholemeal Bread, Ocean Fish, Chicken, Eggs, Balsamic vinegar, brown sugar, peanut

Highly Acidic

Artificial Sweeteners, Syrup, Alcohol, Coffee & Black Tea, Fruit Juice (Sweetened / Concentrated / Packaged), Cocoa, , Jam, Jelly, Mustard, Miso, Rice Syrup,

Soy Sauce, white Vinegar, Yeast, Dried Fruit, Beef, Farmed Fish, Pork, Shellfish, Cheese, Dairy, Wine, Walnut

Breakfast

Peas, Bean and Asparagus Salad with Poached Egg

Total Time: 20 minutes
Makes 4 Servings

- 12 asparagus, spears trimmed
- 1 cup young broad bean
- 1 cup peas
- 1 cup green beans, trimmed
- 1 cup sugar snap pea, trimmed
- 2 tbsp. fresh mint leaves, chopped

  Dressing
- 4 tbsp. extra virgin olive oil
- 2 tbsp. balsamic vinegar
- 1/4 tsp. white sugar
- 4 free-range eggs, poached
- 1/4 tsp. salt

Into a pot of boiling salted water, cook the peas and beans along with asparagus for about 3 minutes. Drain into a colander and rinse under running water. Transfer into a bowl.

Add mint leaves and toss to mix. Combine in the first 4 dressing ingredients. Slowly mix to blend.

Into a saucepan of boiling water, poach the eggs individually. Serve salad into 4 serving plates and top each with poach eggs.

Lunch

Fig and Arugula Salad

Total time: 15 minutes
Makes 4 servings

- 8 fresh figs, quartered
- 4 cups baby arugula
- 1/4 cup cottage cheese, grated
- 2 tbsp. toasted chestnuts

- 2 tbsp. raw honey
- 2 tbsp. apple cider vinegar

Into a large bowl, combine arugula, figs, cheese, and chestnuts together in a large bowl; mix to blend. Upon serving, drizzle vinegar and honey all over the salad. Enjoy.

Dinner

Braised Green Beans with Fried Tofu

Makes 4 servings
Total time: 40 minutes

- 1 (14 oz.) pack tofu, drained, patted dry, cubed
- salt and pepper to taste
- 1 tbsp. arrow root powder
- 3 cups coconut oil, for deep frying
- 1 onion, chopped
- 4 plum tomatoes, sliced into thin wedges
- 12 oz. fresh green beans, trimmed and cut into 3 inch pieces

- 1 cup bamboo shoots, drained and sliced
- 1 cup vegetable broth
- 2 tbsp. arrowroot powder, dissolved in 3 tbsp. water

The Sauce
- 2 tbsp. white sugar
- 3 tbsp. soy sauce
- 1 cup dry white wine
- 1/2 cup vegetable broth

Into a bowl, sprinkle salt and pepper on tofu. Drizzle arrowroot starch and toss to fully coat.

Prepare a deep fryer or a sauce pan with 1 inch oil. Heat oil until its temperature reaches 375 °F. Cook tofu with stirring until all sides are golden brown. Drain on paper towel-lined plate.

Into another pan, heat 1 tbsp. oil over medium high flame and stir fry onions and green beans for about 4 minutes. Season it with salt and pepper. Mix in tomatoes and cook for another 4 minutes or until they are about to burst. Stir in bamboo shoots.

Meanwhile into a bowl, combine all ingredients for the sauce. Mix well to blend.

Pour in the sauce into the pan and heat to boil. Cook and stir for 5 minutes longer, adding more vegetable broth to keep the moisture. Add in previously dissolved arrowroot starch in water and stir. Lower heat and simmer for about 3 minutes or until thickened. Add in the tofu, slowly mix for the sauce to coat everything.

Serve warm. Enjoy.

Drinks

Watermelon Pineapple and Coriander Cucumber Juice

Total time 10 minutes
Makes 4 servings

- 1 cucumber, chopped

- 1 peeled pineapple, not cored, chopped
- 1 seedless watermelon with the rind chopped
- 15-20 stems of coriander

Rinse well all the ingredients, including the rind of the watermelon. Blend watermelon flesh and set aside. Slide all other ingredients through a juicer. Combine juice with blended watermelon. Serve chilled.

Sides 1

Curried Root Vegetable Soup

Makes 6 servings
Total time: 1 hour 40 minutes

- 2 tbsp. coconut oil
- 6 red radishes, chopped
- 6 turnips, chopped
- 6 green onions, chopped
- 2 heads garlic, chopped
- 5 carrots, peeled and chopped

- 1 1/2 lbs. potatoes, cut into cubes
- 1 quart vegetable broth
- 1 bay leaf
- 1 1/2 cups whole milk
- 3 tbsp. Worcestershire sauce
- 2 tbsp. curry powder
- 10 grinds cracked black pepper

Into a pan, heat oil over medium flame and cook garlic, green onions turnips, and radishes for about 3 minutes. Mix in potatoes, carrots and pour in vegetable broth. Boil and simmer over lower heat. Add bay leaf and cook on low flame for about 45 minutes, with occasional stirring.

Remove from flame, remove and throw away bay leaf. Into a food processor, carefully process the hot mixture in batches, until pureed. Pour into a saucepan and heat over low flame.

Mix in whole milk, curry powder, Worcestershire sauce, and black pepper into the soup; and continue heating for another 15 minutes with constant stirring or until well blended.

Sides 2

Mashed Rutabaga with Milk

Makes 4 servings
Total time: 55 minutes

- 2 lbs. rutabagas, peeled and cubed
- 2 tsp. coconut oil
- 1/4 cup whole milk
- 1 tsp. lemon
- 2 tbsp. fresh dill, chopped
- Sea salt and black pepper

Into a saucepan, cover rutabaga with salted water and boil over medium high flame for about 30 minutes or until tender. Drain into a colander and return to the pan.

Reduce flame to low and steam rutabaga for a minute; while swirling the pan to avoid sticking. Using a potato masher, mash the rutabaga. Mix in the remaining ingredients and mix until well blended. Serve with some additional dill as garnish.

Snacks

Root Vegetable Chips with Greek Yogurt Dip

Makes 6 servings
Total time: 45 minutes

- 4 cups coconut oil for frying, or as needed
- 1 turnip, peeled and thinly sliced
- 1 large beet, peeled and thinly sliced
- 1 golden beet, peeled and thinly sliced
- 1 large sweet potato, peeled and thinly sliced
- 1 parsnip, peeled and thinly sliced
- sea salt to taste
- freshly cracked black pepper to taste
- 1 tbsp. apple cider vinegar
- 1 cup plain Greek yogurt
- 1/4 cup fresh parsley, chopped
- 1 tbsp. chopped fresh mint
- 1 clove garlic, finely minced
- 4 green onions, finely chopped
- 2 tbsp. lemon juice, or to taste
- Sea salt and ground white pepper to taste

Into a large saucepan or deep-fryer, heat oil to 360 º F.

Fry turnip, parsnip, beets, and sweet potato for about 3 minutes per batch. Using a slotted spoon, transfer chips into a paper-lined platter to drain excess oil. Set aside to dry and cool at the same time.

Sprinkle salt and pepper and drizzle vinegar to taste.

Prepare dip by combining yogurt, mint, garlic, parsley, and green onions together into a bowl. Mix in lemon juice and season with salt, and white pepper to taste.

Breakfast

Banana with Cottage Cheese Breakfast

Total Time: 8 minutes
Makes 1 serving

- 1 small cinnamon raisin gluten-free bagel or wheat bread
- 1 medium banana, sliced
- 1/4 cup cottage cheese
- 1 tbsp. stevia
- 1 dash ground cinnamon

Into a toaster, toast bagel, or bread. Put banana slices on top, and spread cottage cheese on top. Drizzle stevia and cinnamon all over the top.

Lunch

Chicken Salad with Fruits and Veggies

Makes 4 servings
Total time: 20 minutes

- 4 cups mixed salad greens
- 1 lbs. cooked chicken breast, deboned, chopped
- 1/2 cup avocado, peeled, pitted and diced
- 1 cup fresh mango, diced
- 1 cup pineapple chunks
- 1 (15 oz.) can black beans, rinsed and drained
- 1/2 cup green bell pepper, chopped
- 1/2 cup Cheddar cheese, shredded
- 1/4 cup almond nuts, toasted

For the Dressing
- 1/2 tbsp. olive oil
- 1 tbsp. sesame oil
- 1/4 cup orange juice
- 1/4 cup unsweetened pineapple juice
- 1/2 tbsp. fresh parsley, chopped

- 1 tbsp. fresh lime juice
- 1 tbsp. light soy sauce
- 1 tsp. raw honey
- 1 tsp. ground black pepper

Into a bowl, whisk together fruit juices, parsley, lime juice, soy sauce, sesame oil, olive oil, honey and pepper.

Into a large salad bowl, combine salad greens with previously mixed dressing ingredients. Toss to coat. Divide salad into 4 plates, and place chicken on tops. Arrange all the other ingredients aesthetically around the salad greens.

Dinner

Sautéed Kale and Broccoli with Tomatoes

Makes 6 servings
Total time: 10 minutes

- 2 tbsp. virgin olive oil
- 1 chilli pepper, chopped
- 7 cloves garlic, sliced
- 1 head fresh broccoli, chopped
- 1 bunch kale, stems removed and chopped
- 1/4 cup sun-dried tomatoes, cut in thin strips
- 2 limes, juiced

Into a skillet, heat oil over high flame and cook garlic and chilli pepper for about 2 minutes with stirring. Mix in broccoli and cook for 1 minute. Add kale and cook for another 2 minutes. Lastly, add tomatoes, stir and cook for about a minute or until about to burst. Drizzle lemon juice and season with salt and pepper to taste. Enjoy.

Drinks

Blackberry Beet Juice with Apple and Ginger

Makes 4 servings
Total time 10 minutes

- 3 beets
- 1 cup blackberries
- 1 small ginger root, peeled
- 3 apples, cored, chopped

Process all ingredients through a juicer. Serve over ice or chilled.

Sides 1

Rutabaga Fries

Makes 4 servings
Total time: 40 minutes
- 1 rutabaga, peeled and cut lengthwise
- 1 tsp. olive oil
- 3 cloves garlic, minced
- 4 sprigs fresh rosemary, minced
- 1 pinch salt to taste

Preheat oven to 400 °F.

Into a baking sheet, combine all ingredients. Toss well

to blend. Evenly spread onto the sheet in single layer and with ample spaces in between the spears.

Roast for about 30 minutes or until golden brown and crisp. Serve immediately.

Sides 2

Sweet Potato and Apple Casserole

Makes 4 servings
Total time: 1 hour 10 minutes

- 3/4 cup sweet potato, peeled, cubed
- 3 apples cored, sliced
- 2 tbsp. coconut oil
- 1 tbsp. ground cinnamon
- ½ tsp. ground nutmeg
- ¼ cup coconut sugar
- Salt and Pepper to taste

Preheat oven to 374 °F.

Into a pot, place 1 quart water and ½ teaspoon salt and bring to boil over high heat. Boil potatoes for about 15 minutes or until fork tender. Decant and set aside the potatoes.

Into a saucepan, heat oil over medium heat and sauté apple slices for about 10 minutes until tender.

Into a bowl, combine sweet potatoes and apples, season with salt and pepper. Stir in coconut sugar, toss until well coated. Place the mixture into a 2 quart baking dish and bake for about 30 minutes. Cool for about 5 minutes before serving.

Snacks

Toasted Pumpkin Seeds

Makes 2 cups
Total time: 1 hour 10 minutes

- 2 cups raw pumpkin seeds, rinsed, patted dry
- 1 1/2 tsp. Worcestershire sauce

- 1 1/2 tbsp. coconut oil, melted
- 1 1/4 tsp. sea salt

Preheat the oven to 250 °F.

Into a bowl, combine pumpkin seeds with Worcester-shire sauce, melted coconut oil and seasoned with sea salt. Evenly spread seeds onto a baking sheet and bake for about an hour or until crisp and golden brown. Stir once in a while.

Breakfast

Blueberry and Green Tea Smoothie

Total Time: 10 minutes
Makes 2 Servings

- 2 green tea bags, brewed overnight
- 3/4 cup boiling water
- 2 cups frozen blueberries
- 3 ice cubes
- 12 oz. non-fat vanilla yogurt
- 2 tbsp. almonds, whole dry-roasted, unsalted
- 2 tbsp. flax seeds, ground

Drop tea bags into boiling water and steep for about 4 minutes. Squeeze tea bags and discard. Cover and refrigerate tea overnight.

The next morning, into a blender, combine tea, blueberries, flaxseed, yogurt, almonds and ice cubes. Blend until smooth.

Lunch

Tofu "Lasagna" with Grilled Vegetables

Total time: 1 hour 20 minutes
Makes 6 servings

For the marinade:
- 3/4 cup virgin olive oil
- 6 strips lemon zest
- 1/3 cup fresh lemon juice
- 3 garlic cloves, crushed
- salt and freshly ground pepper

For the pesto:
- 1/2 cup pine nuts, toasted
- 1 small garlic clove, smashed
- 2 cups fresh basil
- 1/2 cup virgin olive oil
- salt and freshly ground pepper

For the "lasagna":
- 1 (14 oz.) pack extra-firm tofu, thickly sliced

lengthwise, patted dry

- 2 1/2 lbs. zucchini and yellow summer squashes, thinly sliced lengthwise
- virgin olive oil, for brushing
- salt and freshly ground pepper
- 2 medium tomatoes, sliced 1/4 inch thick
- 18 large basil leaves

Into a skillet, combine lemon zest, oil and garlic; heat over medium flame until bubbly. Mix in lemon juice, salt and pepper to taste. Set aside marinade.

Into a food processor, combine pine nuts and garlic; process until paste. Add basil leaves and pulse until well combined. While processing, slowly pour in oil until smooth. Add salt and pepper to taste. Set aside pesto.

Preheat grill to medium.

Into a bowl, combine vegetable slices with oil, mix until well coated. Season with salt and pepper. Grill for about 8 minutes, flipping sides until lightly charred.

Transfer into a bowl. Whisk marinade and drizzle half of it into the grilled vegetables.

Grill tofu this time for about 3 minutes, flipping side occasionally, until nicely charred. Cool a bit and slice into 1/8-inch-thick.

Place 3 slices each of the veggies on a plate, forming a rectangle. Scoop 3 tbsp. pesto and spread on top. Place a layer of tofu on top of the pesto and another layer of tomatoes, and season it with salt and pepper. Finally top everything with basil leaves. Repeat layering for other servings.

Dinner

Celery Root Salad

Makes 6 servings
Total time: 45 minutes

- 1 large celery root with leaves, halved, peeled, thinly sliced
- 1/4 cup fresh cilantro, chopped

- 3 tbsp. pecans, chopped
- 1/3 cup mayonnaise
- 1/2 lemon, zested and juiced
- 1/4 tsp. ground coriander
- 1/4 tsp. celery seed
- 1/4 tsp. salt (optional)

Into a salad bowl, combine cilantro, pecans and celery root and its leaves. Into another bowl, whisk lemon zest, mayonnaise, lemon juice, coriander, and celery seed; season with salt. Pour dressing into the salad and toss to blend.

Place inside the fridge, covered for at least 30 minutes. Serve.

Drinks

Fresh Fruit and Veggie Juice

Makes 2 servings
Total time 10 minutes

- 1/2 green apple, cored
- 1/2 large green pear, cored
- 2 large carrots
- 2 talks of celery
- 1/2 cucumber
- 2 stalks of kale
- 1 stalk of broccoli
- 1 chunk of cauliflower
- 1/4 beet, peeled
- 1 tomato
- small bit of parsley

Rinse well all fruits and veggies. Run through the juicer. Serve chilled or with ice cubes.

Sides 1

Potato, Parsnip and Rutabaga Casserole with Caramelized Onions

Makes 8 servings
Total time:

- 7 cups low-sodium vegetable broth
- 3 lbs. baking potatoes, peeled and cubed
- 1 1/4 lbs. parsnips, peeled and cubed
- 1 1/2 lbs. rutabagas, peeled and cubed
- 8 cloves garlic
- 1 bay leaf
- 1 tsp. dried thyme
- 3/4 cup coconut oil, softened
- 3 onions, thinly sliced
- salt and ground black pepper to taste

Into a large pot, combine chicken broth with garlic, bay leaf, thyme, potatoes, parsnips and rutabagas. Mix and bring to a boil over high flame. Lower heat and simmer for about 30 minutes or until vegetables are fork tender. Drain into a colander and transfer into a large bowl. Discard bay leaf.

Add 1/2 cup coconut oil into the bowl of cooked vegetables and using a hand mixer, process until mashed and yet chunky. Sprinkle salt and pepper to taste. Spread mixture into a lightly greased baking dish.

Meanwhile, into a pan, heat remaining coconut oil over

medium high flame and cook onions for about 5 minutes or until translucent. Reduce heat to low and continue cooking the onions for about 15 minutes or until golden brown. Season it with salt and pepper to taste.

Evenly spread caramelized onions on top of the mashed vegetable in the baking dish and bake in preheated oven at 375 °F for about 25 minutes or until starting to crisp.

Sides 2

Creamy Mashed Turnips

Makes 6 servings
Total time: 30 minutes

- 3 lbs. turnips, peeled, cubed
- 6 black peppercorns
- 6 whole cloves
- 2 bay leaves
- 1 tbsp. plus 1 tsp. sea salt
- 1/2 cup heavy cream

- 2 tbsp. unsalted butter
- 1 tsp. white pepper
- freshly grated nutmeg to taste

Into a pot, cover turnips with enough water. Into a piece of cheesecloth, combine peppercorns, cloves and bay leaves. Wrap and secure with a kitchen string. Drop into the pot and bring to a boil over medium high flame for about 18 minutes or until tender. Drain into a colander, discard the bag with spices.

Place back turnips into the pot and mix in cream and butter. Bring to a simmer over low flame. Slowly transfer into a blender. Add in white pepper, salt and nutmeg, blend until pureed. Serve at once.

Snacks

Coconut Chia Seed Crispy Balls

Makes 4 servings
Total time: 25 minutes

- 1 cup coconut flour
- 1 tsp. arrowroot powder
- 1/2 cup chia seeds
- 1 1/2 tsp. garlic powder
- 1 tsp. sea salt
- 1/2 cup water
- 1 pinch garlic salt

Preheat oven to 350 ° F.

Into a bowl, combine chia seeds, coconut flour, arrowroot powder, garlic powder and sea salt. Mix well. Gradually add water until dough is formed. Set aside for about 5 minutes for flour to absorb moisture. Add more water if needed to form a dough.

Form bite-size dough balls and arrange on a baking sheet. Sprinkle balls with garlic powder and some salt. Bake for about 15 minutes or until golden brown and crisp. Cool totally and store in an airtight container.

Breakfast

Veggie Hash with Eggs

Total Time: 30 minutes
Makes 2 Servings

- 1 tbsp. virgin olive oil
- 2 tbsp. butter
- 1/4 cup sweet white onion, chopped
- 2 garlic cloves, minced
- 1 cup yellow squash, chopped
- 1/2 cup mushroom, sliced
- salt and pepper
- 1 cup cherry tomatoes, halved
- 1 cup fresh spinach, chopped
- 4 free range eggs, poached
- 1 avocado, sliced

Into a pan, heat oil and butter over medium heat. Cook garlic and onions for about 2 seconds or until tender. Mix in squash, cook for another 2 minutes or until just tender. Add in mushrooms, cook further for another 5 minutes or until just wilted. Season it with salt and pepper to taste.

Stir in spinach and tomatoes, cook for another 30 seconds or until just saggy. Turn off heat and scoop veggies into individual plates without the generated liquid.

Meanwhile poach the eggs into desired doneness. Place 2 eggs on top of the veggies. Serve with avocado slices and a favourite tea.

Lunch

Kale salad with Apple, Avocado, and Bacon bits

Makes 2 servings
Total time: 20 minutes

Salad:
- 2 green apples, thinly sliced
- 1/2 lemon, juiced

- 6 cups kale, thinly sliced
- 4 slices cooked uncured bacon, crumbled
- 1/2 avocado, thinly sliced
- 1/4 cup almonds, chopped

Dressing:
- 1/4 cup apple cider vinegar
- 1/2 cup olive oil
- 2 tbsp. maple syrup
- 2 tsp. grainy mustard
- 1 tsp. ground black pepper
- 1/2 tsp. kosher salt

Immediately toss freshly cut apples with lemon juice. Mix in bacon, avocado, kale and almonds. Into a separate bowl, combine maple syrup, mustard, pepper, olive oil, vinegar, and salt; mix to blend. Pour dressing into the salad, toss to coat.

Dinner

Stir-fried Vegetable with Tofu

Makes 2 servings
Total time:

- 1 tbsp. coconut oil
- 1/2 medium onion, sliced
- 2 cloves garlic, finely chopped
- 1 tbsp. fresh ginger root, finely chopped
- 1 (16 oz.) pack tofu, drained, cubed
- 1/2 cup water
- 4 tbsp. apple cider vinegar
- 2 tbsp. honey
- 2 tbsp. soy sauce
- 2 tsp. arrowroot starch dissolved in 2 tbsp. water
- 1 carrot, peeled and sliced
- 1 green bell pepper, seeded and cut into strips
- 1 cup baby corn, drained and cut into pieces
- 1 small head bok choy, chopped
- 2 cups fresh mushrooms, chopped

- 1 1/4 cups bean sprouts
- 1 cup bamboo shoots, drained and chopped
- 1/2 tsp. crushed red pepper
- 2 medium green onions, thinly sliced diagonally

Into a large wok, heat oil over medium high flame. Sauté onions for a minute. Mix in ginger and garlic, stir fry for 30 seconds. Mix in tofu; stir and cook until golden brown.

Mix in baby corn, carrots, and bell pepper and cook for another 2 minutes. Stir in bamboo shoots, mushrooms, bok choy, bean sprouts, and crushed red pepper, mix and cook for about a minute or until well heated through. Put off heat.

Into a small pan, mix apple cider vinegar, with water, honey, and soy sauce, heat and a simmer for two minutes, stir in arrowroot and water mixture; cook further until thickened. Pour sauce over tofu-vegetables mix. Serve garnished with scallions.

Drinks

Pineapple Mint Juice with Apples

Makes 1 serving

Total time 10 minutes

- ½ pineapple, peeled and chopped
- 1 green apple, cored
- 2 handfuls fresh mint

Process all ingredients through a juicer; add equal parts of clean water. Serve over ice or chilled.

Sides 1

Chicken Soup with Root Vegetables

Makes 6 servings

Total time: 3 hours 40 minutes

- 1 roasted chicken, cut into pieces
- 12 cups cold water
- 3 stalks celery, chopped

- 2 carrots, chopped
- 1 onion, chopped
- 1/4 bunch parsley
- 2 bay leaves
- 12 whole black peppercorns
- 2 tbsp. olive oil
- 1 red onion, chopped
- 2 stalks celery, diced
- 2 carrots, diced
- 1 large parsnip, peeled and diced
- 1/2 lb. rutabaga, peeled and diced
- 2 cloves garlic, minced
- 2 tbsp. minced parsley
- salt and black pepper to taste
- 1 cup uncooked orzo pasta

Into a pot, combine chicken meat with 12 cups water and bring to a boil over high heat. Skim off any fat that forms on top. Mix in chopped onion, chopped celery, chopped carrots, , 1/4 bunch of parsley, peppercorns and bay leaves. Continue simmering uncovered for about 3 hours. Strain chicken broth into a bowl.

Into a skillet, heat oil over medium high flame. Cook red onions for about 5 minutes or until translucent and tender. Mix in rutabaga, diced carrots, diced celery, and parsnip; cook for another 5 minutes more.

Add chopped parsley and the garlic, and cook for another minute more. Pour in the chicken broth, sprinkle salt and pepper to taste, and heat over high flame to simmer for about 20 minutes until tender. Add orzo pasta and continue cooking for another 7 minutes or until pasta just softened. Cover and put off heat; let stand for 5 minutes before serving.

Sides 2

Baked Sweet Potato

Makes 2 servings
Total time: 1 hour

- 2 medium sweet potato
- Salt and pepper to taste
- Fresh dill, chopped

Preheat oven to 450 °F. Line a cookie sheet with tin foil.

Wash well sweet potato under running water and dry using paper towel. Poke potatoes all over with fork. Place sweet potatoes on cookie sheet and bake for about 30 minutes. Flip over and cook for another 25 minutes or until fork tender. Remove and scrape off any blackened particles from the leaking juices.

Let cool for about 5 minutes and cut into serving sizes. Season with salt and pepper to taste. Garnish with dill.

Snacks

Roasted Root Vegetable Cubes

Makes 8 servings
Total Time: 40 Minutes

- 6 whole carrots, peeled and diced
- 1 whole celery root, peeled and diced
- 3 whole parsnips, peeled and diced

- 2 rutabaga, peeled and diced
- olive oil, for drizzling
- salt and pepper, to taste

Preheat oven to 375 °F.

Into a large baking sheet, spread all cubed root vegetables. Drizzle with olive oil and sprinkle with salt and pepper to taste. Evenly spread in one layer and bake for about 35 minutes or until they turn golden brown. Cool and enjoy.

Day 5

Breakfast

Orange Flaxseed Smoothie

Total Time: 12 minutes
Makes 1 Serving

- 1 navel orange, white pith removed, seeded
- 1 tsp. orange zest

- 1/2 cup plain low-fat yogurt
- 2/3 cup frozen blueberries
- 1/2 cup apple, chopped
- 3 ice cubes
- 1 tbsp. honey
- 2 tbsp. ground flax seed

Into a blender, combine all ingredients, process until smooth.

Pour into a tall glass and enjoy. Serve with steamed broccoli florets.

Lunch

Broccoli and Brussels Sprout with Rice

Makes 4 servings
Total time: 25 minutes

- 3 tbsp. coconut oil, divided
- 2 cloves garlic, chopped
- 2 cups broccoli florets

- 8 Brussels sprouts, trimmed and halved
- 1 small tomato, seeded and diced
- 1/4 tsp. salt
- 1/8 tsp. red pepper flakes
- 2 cups steamed white rice

Into a wok, heat 1 tbsp. oil over medium flame. Cook garlic for about 2 minutes or until aromatic. Add remaining oil and mix in brussel sprouts, tomatoes and broccoli; sprinkle salt and pepper flakes to taste.

Put cover and cook for about 5 minutes or until veggies are lightly browned. Turn sides and cook covered for another 4 minutes.

Serve with half a cup of steamed rice per serving.

Dinner

Spinach Cantaloupe Salad with Mint

Makes 2 servings
Total time: 15 minutes

- 1 cup avocado, thickly sliced
- 4 cups fresh young spinach leaves
- 1 cup cantaloupe, thickly sliced
- 1/2 cup red bell pepper, diced
- 2 tbsp. fresh mint leaves, chopped
- 1 tbsp. mint apple jelly
- 1 1/2 tsp. apple cider vinegar
- 3 tbsp. coconut oil
- 1 clove garlic, minced

Equally divide the spinach onto 2 plates. Arrange avocado and cantaloupe slices around them, sprinkle red pepper and fresh mint on tops.

Make the dressing by combining apple cider vinegar with mint apple jelly, oil and garlic. Whisk until blended. Drizzle over the salad and serve.

Drinks

Dragon Fruit Juice Blend

Makes 1 serving
Total time 10 minutes

- 1/2 cup dragon fruit, peeled and coarsely chopped
- 1 orange, peeled and segmented
- 1/4 cup fresh basil juice from
- 1/2 a lime

Process everything through a juicer. Drink and enjoy.

Sides 1

Cauliflower Mash with Garlic and Chives

Makes 4 Servings
Total time; 15 minutes

- 4 cups cauliflower florets

- 1/3 cup mayonnaise
- 1/2 tsp. sea salt
- 1/8 tsp. black pepper
- 1 clove garlic, peeled
- 1 tbsp. water
- 1/4 tsp. lemon juice
- 1/2 tsp. lemon zest
- 1 tbsp. fresh chives, chopped

Into a microwavable bowl, mix cauliflower with garlic, mayonnaise, salt and pepper along with water. Heat in the oven on high for about 13 minutes or until tender. Transfer into the food processor and process until pureed. Add lemon juice and its zest along with chives; pulse until well blended. Serve warm.

Sides 2

Baked Potato Fries with Cumin and Cayenne Pepper

Makes 2 servings
Total time: 40 minutes

- 3 1/3 cups potatoes cut into shoe-string fries
- 3 tbsp. virgin olive oil
- 1 1/2 tsp. coconut sugar
- 1 1/2 tsp. salt
- 1/4 tsp. cumin
- 1/4 tsp. chilli powder
- 1/8 tsp. cayenne pepper

Preheat the oven to 425 °F.

Into a bowl, mix oil with the rest of the ingredients. Add potatoes, toss all together until thoroughly coated.

Evenly spread on a cookie sheet and bake for about 30 minutes or until brown and crisp, turning once.

Snacks

Root Vegetable Gratin Recipe

Makes 4 servings
Total time:

- 2 potatoes, peeled and sliced thinly
- 2 sweet potatoes, peeled and sliced thinly
- 1 celery root, peeled and sliced thinly
- 1 1/4 cup cottage cheese, divided
- 1/2 cup almond flour
- 2 cups whole milk
- 2 tsp. red chilli flakes
- salt and freshly ground pepper
- 3 cloves garlic, minced
- 1 cup scallions, chopped

Preheat oven to 375 °F. Lightly grease a 9 inch baking dish.

Into a small saucepan combine the milk with, garlic, chillies and scallions; bring to a simmer over medium flame. Mix in half of the cheese and some salt. Put off heat and set aside.

Into the bottom of prepared baking dish, layer sweet potatoes. Sprinkle 1 tbsp. almond flour and pour in third of the milk mixture. Layer potatoes this time and sprinkle again top with flour and pour another 1/3 of the milk mixture. Lastly, layer rutabaga, more flour and remaining milk mixture. Dot top with cottage cheese.

Cover dish with tin foil and bake for about 55 minutes. At the last 10 minutes of baking, remove the tin foil. Cool on wire rack and serve.

Breakfast

Berry Breakfast Power Bar

Total Time: 40 minutes
Makes 16 Servings

- 1 1/2 cups dessert apples, chopped
- 1 oz. dried unsweetened cranberries
- 1 oz. dried unsweetened blueberries
- 2 tbsp. lemon juice
- 1/2 cup coconut oil
- 1/3 cup white sugar
- 4 cups rolled oats
- 3 tbsp. oat bran
- 1/3 cup ground flax seeds
- 1 oz. sesame seeds
- 3 tbsp. sunflower seeds
- 1/3 cup brazil nuts (shaved)

Preheat oven to 375 °F.

Into a saucepan, bring 1 cup water into a boil and cook apples. Bring down heat to simmer for about 10 minute or until tender. Set aside.

Into another pan, combine coconut oil with sugar. Add ½ cup water and boil. Mix in berries and simmer for about 2 minutes or until plumped up. Combine the rest of the ingredients along with the apples. Put off heat and mix.

Spread mixture into 8 x 12 inch baking pan and bake for about 25 minutes. Cool on wire rack and slice to desired cuts.

Lunch

Swiss Chard with Pinto Beans Casserole

Makes 4 servings
Total Time: 38 minutes

- 3 tbsp. coconut oil, divided
- 2 cloves garlic, minced

- 1 pinch red pepper flakes
- 1 bunch Swiss chard, rinsed, stems cut into 1/2 inch slices
- 1 (15.5 oz.) can pinto beans, rinsed and drained
- 1 small tomato, chopped
- salt and pepper to taste
- 1 tbsp. fresh lime juice
- 3 tbsp. goat cheese

Preheat oven to 350 °F. Lightly grease a 9 inch square baking dish.

Into a large pan, heat oil over medium heat; cook and stir pepper flakes and garlic for about a minute or until aromatic. Add in Swiss chard and cook, covered for about 4 minutes. Mix in pinto beans, tomato, and lime juice; add salt and pepper to taste. Put cover and continue cooking for another 4 minutes or until chard is just wilted.

Transfer chard mixture into prepared baking dish, sprinkle goat cheese all over the top bake for about 15 minutes or until cheese melts.

Dinner

Chickpea Curry with Turnips

Makes 4 servings
Total time: 2 hours 5 minutes

- 2 tbsp. olive oil
- 2 cloves garlic, minced
- 1/2 onion, diced
- 2 tbsp. curry powder
- 1 tbsp. ground cumin
- 1 (15 oz.) can chickpeas, un-drained
- 1/2 red bell pepper, diced
- 1 turnip, peeled and diced
- 1 cup corn kernels
- 1/2 (15 oz.) can tomato sauce
- 1 pinch crushed red pepper flakes
- 1 pinch salt
- 1 pinch cracked black pepper

Into a skillet, heat oil over medium flame until shimmering. Cook and stir onion, cumin, garlic and curry for about 5 minutes or until tender. Mix in chickpeas and its liquid, turnip, red bell peppers, corn kernel and tomato sauce. Sprinkle salt and pepper to taste. Heat and simmer over medium-low flame for about 2 hours or until veggies are tender and sauce has thickened.

Drinks

Green Cleaner Juice Recipe

Total time 10 minutes
Makes 1 serving

- Half a head of romaine lettuce
- 2 sticks celery
- ½ cucumber
- 1 green apple, cored
- 2 stalks kale
- Handful of parsley
- 1 lemon, peeled

Process all ingredients through juicer. Strain away solids. Serve over ice or chilled.

Sides 1

Garlic Ginger Tofu

Makes 8 servings
Total time: 15 minutes

- 3 tbsp. canola oil
- 2 tsp. fresh ginger root, minced
- 2 tsp. garlic, minced
- 1 lime
- 1 tbsp. coconut amino, or to taste
- 2 lbs. firm tofu, cubed

Into a skillet, heat oil over medium flame. Cook ginger and garlic for about a minute. Mix in tofu and coconut amino, cover and cook for another 25 minutes or until tofu is well cooked.

Drizzle lime juice and serve with main dish.

Sides 2

Smashed Sweet Potato

Makes 2 servings
Total time: 5 minutes

- 2 medium-sized sweet potato, peeled, roasted
- coconut oil

Heat coconut oil into a pan over medium-high. Put the roasted sweet potato in the pan, press flat with a fork or spatula. Fry on each side for about 3 minutes or until the sweet potato caramelizes. Transfer into a plate.

Snacks

Baked Veggie Chips

Makes 6 servings
Total time: 45 minutes

- 2 sweet potatoes, peeled and thinly sliced
- 2 large parsnips, peeled, trimmed, thinly sliced
- 1 celery root, peeled and sliced thinly
- 2 purple or golden beets, peeled and sliced thinly
- sea salt

Preheat oven to 375 °F. Lightly grease 2 baking sheets.

Into a large bowl put all the vegetable slices and sprinkle salt to taste. Toss to mix. Onto a paper-lined baking sheet, lay flat all the vegetable slices and set aside for about 15 minutes. Blot dry after set time.

Spread in 1 layer the vegetable slice on prepared baking sheets. Bake in upper and lower thirds of the preheated oven for about 20 minutes or until crisp. Work in batches if needed. Sprinkle more salt to taste then cool on wire rack.

Breakfast

Quinoa Fruit Salad

Total Time: 10 minutes
Makes 4 Servings

- 2 apples, roughly chopped
- 2 pears, roughly chopped
- 1 banana, thickly sliced
- 3/4 cup quinoa
- 1/2 cup almond cereal
- 1 tsp. cinnamon
- Stevia sugar substitute (optional)

Into a saucepan, combine quinoa with 1 cup water. Bring to boil and simmer for about 15 minutes or until most of the water is absorbed. Set aside for about 5 minutes to cool. Fluff with a fork.

Into a bowl, mix half of the quinoa along with the fruits

and yogurt. Add sweetener and mix. Drizzle remaining quinoa on top and sprinkle some cinnamon.

Lunch

Tempeh Tacos

Makes 4 servings
Total time: 30 minutes

- 2 tbsp. virgin olive oil
- 2 cloves garlic, minced
- 1 small onion, minced
- 1 (8 oz.) pack spicy tempeh, coarsely grated
- 1/2 cup vegetable broth
- 2 tbsp. taco seasoning mix
- 1 tsp. dried oregano
- 1/2 tsp. ground red pepper (optional)

Into a pan, heat oil over medium high flame and cook onion for about 5 minutes or until just tender. Mix in garlic, cook for another 2 minutes or until aromatic. Stir in tempeh; cook for another 5 minutes or until golden brown.

Pour in vegetable broth, simmer over lower temperature with ground red pepper, taco seasoning, and oregano for about 5 minutes more or until most of the liquid is gone.

Dinner

Kale Salad with Alfalfa Sprouts and Pumpkin Seeds

Makes 6 servings
Total time: 1 hour 30 minutes

- 1/2 cup soy sauce
- 1/2 cup lemon juice
- 1/2 cup virgin olive oil
- 1 red onion, halved and sliced
- 1 cup alfalfa sprouts
- 5 bunches kale leaves, torn into bite-size pieces
- 1/3 cup sunflower kernels
- 1/3 cup pumpkin seeds, hulled
- 1/4 cup sesame seeds

Into a bowl, combine coconut aminos with olive oil and lemon juice; whisk until smooth. Add red onions and alfalfa sprouts; mix to evenly coat. Cover and set aside for about 15 minutes to marinate.

Into a mixing bowl, combine, kale with pumpkin seeds, sunflower kernels and sesame seeds. Mix in dressing and toss to evenly blend. Chill covered for an hour, and serve.

Drinks

Strawberry-Kiwi Juice

Makes 4 servings
Total time 10 minutes

- 2 kiwifruit, peeled
- 4 cups strawberry
- 1 cup water
- 2 tbsp. fresh lime juice
- 3 tbsp. honey

Slide kiwifruit and strawberries into the chute of a juicer and process. Add water, lime juice and honey; stir and serve chilled.

Sides 1

Mushroom and Swiss Chard Salad

Makes 2 servings
Total Time: 25 minutes

- 1 tbsp. olive oil
- 2 cloves garlic, minced
- 1 bunch Swiss chard, cut into thin strips
- 10 cremini mushrooms, sliced
- 1/4 cup chopped onion
- 3 tbsp. balsamic vinegar
- 12 grape tomatoes, quartered
- 2 tbsp. blue cheese, crumbled
- 1 pinch salt and ground black pepper to taste

Into a skillet, heat oil over medium high flame until shimmering. Cook garlic for about a minute or until aromatic and light browned. Stir in Swiss chard and cook for about 4 minutes or until just wilted. Using a slotted spoon, transfer chard into a bowl.

Into the same pan and generated juice, cook onions and mushrooms over medium flame for about 3 minutes. Pour in balsamic vinegar, stir and cook for 3 minutes more. Combine with the chard into the bowl. Add tomatoes and blue cheese, toss to blend. Sprinkle salt and pepper to taste and serve.

Sides 2

Lemony Carrot Salad

Makes 4 servings
Total time: 30 minutes

- 2 cups carrots, grated
- 2 tbsp. lemon juice
- 2 tbsp. extra-virgin olive oil
- 1 small clove garlic, minced
- 1/4 tsp. sea salt, or to taste

- freshly ground pepper, to taste
- 3 tbsp. fresh dill, chopped
- 2 tbsp. scallions, chopped

Into a bowl, combine oil, lemon juice, garlic, salt and pepper; whisk to blend. Add carrots, scallions and dill; toss to coat. Cover with plastic wrap, chill for about 30 minutes and serve.

Snacks

Spinach Quiche

Makes 4 servings
Total time: 30 minutes

- Smoked sun-dried tomatoes, sliced
- 2 avocados, peeled, halved and thinly sliced
- 1/3 cup, smoked sun-dried tomatoes, julienned
- 2 tbsp. red onion, diced
- 2 cups baby spinach
- 4 (4-oz.) mixed grain rye bread, split in half

Into a non-stick lightly greased pan, toast bread to desired doneness.

Layer ½ cup spinach, avocado slices, onion, and tomatoes, on each roll and top with another slice of toasted bread.

Day 8

Breakfast

Herbed Egg Salad with Arugula

Total Time: 25 minutes
Makes 8 Serving

- 8 hard-boiled eggs, finely chopped
- 1 cup fresh herbs, finely chopped (parsley, dill, tarragon, chervil or chives)
- 1 small red onion, finely chopped
- 2 celery ribs, finely chopped
- salt & freshly ground black pepper to taste
- 1 tbsp. apple cider vinegar
- 2 tbsp. fresh lemon juice
- 1/3 cup plain low-fat yogurt
- 1 tbsp. mayonnaise
- 1 garlic clove, green shoot removed, minced
- 1 tbsp. Dijon mustard
- 2 tbsp. extra virgin olive oil
- 6 oz. bag baby arugula

Into a large bowl, combine eggs with herbs, onions and celery. Sprinkle salt and pepper to taste.

Into another bowl, combine the rest of the ingredients but the arugula. Whisk until fully blended. Season to taste with salt and pepper. Pour into the egg mixture, toss to blend.

Line serving plates with the arugula and top each with the egg salad. Enjoy.

Lunch

Pork and Haricot Beans and Greens

Makes 6 servings
Total time: 1 hour 15 minutes

- 2 tsp. salt
- 1 tsp. ground black pepper
- 1 tsp. ground cumin
- 1/2 tsp. dried rosemary
- 1/2 tsp. fennel seeds

- 1/2 tsp. red pepper flakes
- 1/2 tsp. dried oregano
- 2 cloves garlic, sliced
- 1 1/2 tbsp. honey
- 1 tbsp. apple cider vinegar
- 1 tbsp. olive oil
- 4 lbs. boneless pork shoulder roast, trimmed, cubed
- 1 tbsp. olive oil
- 2 cloves garlic, sliced
- 1 (14 oz.) jar white haricot beans, drained and rinsed
- salt to taste
- 1 pinch red pepper flakes, or to taste
- 1 lemon, juiced
- 2 tbsp. vegetable stock
- 1 large bunch of fully grown arugula leaves

Preheat oven to 350 °F.

Into a mortar and pestle, grind the rosemary, fennel, cumin, oregano, red pepper flakes, and salt, black pepper until coarsely ground. Combine in garlic and smashed to a paste. Add in honey, apple cider vinegar, and 1 tbsp. olive oil; mix until thoroughly blended. Into a roasting pan, evenly coat pork with the seasoning paste; bake for about an hour. Flip meat to exposed its other side and roast further for another 30 minutes or until crust turned golden brown. Set aside on a platter, loosely covered with a tin foil to remain warm.

Into a pan, heat oil over medium flame until shimmering and cook cloves of garlic for about a minute or until light browned. Mix in the beans, pepper flakes and salt and pepper to taste; cook for another 4 minutes or until beans are well heated through. Pour in vegetable stock and lemon juice; bring to a slow boil. Add in arugula and cook for another minute or until arugula just wilted. Put off heat.

Equally divide arugula and beans onto the centre of 6 plates. Place a chunk of scorched pork on tops, drizzle juice over meat and serve.

Dinner

Roasted Root Vegetables

Makes 12 servings
Total time: 1 hour 30 minutes

- 1 lb. rutabaga, peeled and cubed
- 1 lb. parsnips, peeled and cubed
- 1 lb. carrots, peeled and cubed
- 1/8 tsp. salt
- 3 tbsp. coconut oil
- 1 tsp. dried basil
- salt and ground black pepper to taste
- 3 tbsp. fresh parsley, chopped
- Slices of roasted beef

Into a pot of enough boiling salted water, cook ruta-baga for about 5 minutes or until fork tender. Drain into a colander, rinse with running water and set aside in a bowl.

Cook carrots and parsnips in the same way. Chill vegetables for about 15 minutes.

Preheat oven to 425 °F. Oil a rimmed baking dish and preheat for about 5 minutes.

Place chilled vegetables into a large bowl, add basil, salt, and pepper; toss to blend. Place into heated oiled baking dish, toss to coat with the oil and bake for about 30 minutes, flipping sides frequently, until golden brown.

Sprinkle parsley and serve with some slices of roasted beef.

Drinks

Blueberry-Ginger Juice

Makes 5 servings
Total time 10 minutes

- 4 cups blueberries
- 2 inches fresh ginger, peeled

- 1/2 cup sugar
- 1/2 cup water
- 1/4 cup fresh ginger, peeled, coarsely chopped
- 6 (2-inch-long) strips lemon rind
- 2 (10-ounce) bottles club soda, chilled
- Ice cubes

Process blueberries and ginger through a juicer. Discard solids and set aside the juice.

Into a saucepan, combine water, lemon rind, chopped ginger and sugar. Bring to a boil, stir until sugar dissolves. Put off heat and set aside to cool.

Into a pitcher, combine juice with syrup and chill. Upon serving, add club soda, some ice cubes and enjoy.

Sides 1

Eggplant Side Dish

Makes 10 servings

Total time: 1 hour
- 1 eggplant, peeled and cubed
- 1 green bell pepper, seeded and chopped
- 1 tomato, chopped
- 1 onion, chopped
- 1 tsp. stevia
- ¼ tsp. sea salt
- 3 tbsp. coconut oil
- 1 tbsp. red wine vinegar
- 3 tbsp. water

Into a saucepan, combine eggplant with tomato, onion and bell pepper. Into another bowl, whisk oil and vinegar with salt, sugar and water. Pour mixture all over the vegetables. Mix, cover and boil over medium heat for about 15 minutes or until tender.

Serve warm.

Sides 2

Baked Potato Topped Wild Organic Honey and Cinnamon

Makes 1 serving
Total time: 50 minutes

- 1 medium potato
- 1 tsp. coconut oil
- 1/8 tsp. cinnamon
- 1 tsp. wild organic honey

Direction

Preheat oven to 400 °F.

Poke potato several times with fork. Place potato on a rimmed baking sheet lined with foil. Bake until tender, about 45 minutes. Make a slit in the top of the sweet potato, and break open.

Drizzle coconut oil on the potato flesh. Top with the cinnamon and honey. Use a fork to slightly mash the potato and the other ingredients together. Serve immediately.

Snacks

Pan Roasted Brussel Sprouts with Pesto

Makes 4 servings
Total time: 20 minutes

- 2 lbs. Brussel Sprouts, trimmed, rinsed, halved
- ¼ cup olive oil
- 4 garlic cloves, peeled and crushed
- 1 cup vegetable stock
- sea salt and cracked black pepper
- virgin olive oil

For the Pesto:
- 1/2 cup pine nuts
- 4 cups fresh basil or parsley leaves
- 1/2 cup cottage cheese, finely grated
- 1 clove garlic
- Salt and pepper
- 1/2 cup extra-virgin olive oil

Preheat oven to 350 º F.

Into a large pan, heat half of the olive oil over medium low heat. Cook garlic cloves for about 3 minutes and set aside. Place sprouts, flat side down in the pan and cook until golden brown. Flip the sides, pour in half of the stock and cook until softened. Work in batches using remaining oil and stock.

Drizzle with a little extra olive oil and season with salt and pepper.

Prepare the pesto. Into a baking dish, spread pine nuts and roast for about 6 minutes or until golden and fragrant. Stir once. Cool on wire rack.

Into a food processor, combine toasted nuts, cheese, basil, and garlic; sprinkle with salt and pepper to taste. Pulse several times until finely chopped. While processing, gently add in olive oil in a steady flow until smooth.

Serve roasted Brussel sprouts with the pesto.

Breakfast

Seed Baguette with Avocado Spread

Total Time: 19 hours
Makes 2 Servings

For bread
- 1 cup sunflower seeds
- 1 cup flax seeds
- 2 tbsp. virgin olive oil
- 1/2 tsp. cinnamon

For spread
- 1 ripe avocado, peeled, pitted
- 1 clove of garlic, finely chopped
- 2 tbsp. virgin cold-pressed olive oil
- Sea salt and pepper to taste

Into a bowl, soak sunflower seeds with enough water to cover for about 7 hours.

Grin flaxseed into a blender until coarsely powdered. Combine with the soaked sunflower seed along with oil and cinnamon. Mix to blend and form into a baguette. Place inside a 104 °F dehydrator overnight.

Prepare the spread. Into a bowl, mix the avocado with the oil and garlic until smooth. Sprinkle salt and pepper to taste.

Lunch

Kelp and Zucchini Lettuce Wraps with Mango

Makes 2 servings
Total Time: 5 minutes

- 1/2 cup raw kelp noodles
- 1 zucchini, julienned
- 2 radishes, sliced into thin sticks
- 1/2 mango, thinly sliced
- 1/4 cup scallions, chopped
- 1 red bell peppers, sliced
- handful of fresh mint

- baked tofu, sliced lengthwise
- bunch of romaine lettuce leaves
- lime wedges

Ginger soy dipping sauce:
- 3 tbsp. apple cider vinegar
- 4 tbsp. coconut amino
- 1 tsp. fresh ginger, minced
- 1/4 tsp. sesame oil
- 2 tsp. honey
- 1 tsp. lemon juice

Into a bowl, combine, kelp noodles, zucchini, radishes, mango, bell peppers, tofu, scallions and mint. Sprinkle some salt and pepper to taste. Toss to combine.

Spread lettuce leaves and scoop half of the vegetable mixture into the centre. Roll up like a burrito. Make another serving. Alternatively, roughly chop the lettuce and mix with the rest in the bowl.

Whisk the dipping sauce ingredients until well blended. Use as a dip or as a dressing. Serve with lime wedges.

Dinner

Greek Salad with Cottage Cheese

Makes 8 servings
Total time: 1 hour 30 minutes

- 3/4 cup olive oil
- 1/4 cup apple cider vinegar
- 1/4 cup fresh dill, chopped
- salt and ground black pepper to taste
- 1 cup cauliflower, chopped
- 1 cucumber, peeled and diced
- 1 cup broccoli, chopped
- 2 plum tomatoes, diced
- 1/2 red bell pepper, chopped
- 1/4 head red cabbage, shredded
- 1/4 large red onion, diced
- 1/2 green bell pepper, chopped
- 1 (5 oz.) jar green olives, sliced
- 1 (4 oz.) package cottage cheese, crumbled

Prepare dressing by whisking olive oil into a bowl with

dill, apple cider vinegar, salt and pepper until smooth. Set aside.

Into a large salad bowl, combine red cabbage, red onion, red bell pepper, green bell, cauliflower, olives, cucumber, broccoli, plum tomatoes, and cottage cheese. Sprinkle dressing and toss to coat. Cover with plastic wrap and chill for about an hour before serving.

Drinks

Green Lemonade

Makes 2 servings
Total time 10 minutes

- 1 head romaine lettuce
- 4 leaves kale
- 1 (1/2 inch) piece ginger
- 2 apples, quartered
- 1 lemon

Process everything through a juicer. Stir before drinking. Serve chilled if desired.

Sides 1

Potatoes, Arugula and Green Beans with Chestnuts

Makes 6 servings
Total Time: 15 minutes

- 1/3 cup chestnuts
- 1 1/2 lbs. fingerling potatoes, cut crosswise
- 6 oz. haricots, or other green beans, trimmed and cut into 2-inch segments
- 2 tbsp. rice vinegar
- 2 tbsp. plain yogurt
- 1 tsp. Dijon mustard
- 1 tsp. coarse salt
- Freshly ground pepper
- 2 tbsp. olive oil
- 3 oz. baby arugula

Preheat oven to 375°F.

Onto a rimmed baking sheet, spread chestnuts and roast in oven for about 8 minutes or until fragrant. Set aside to cool a bit, then chop coarsely.

Into a large saucepan, bring enough water to a boil over high flame. Add potatoes, and cook for about 10 minutes or until fork tender. Drain potatoes into a colander, rinse with running water and set aside.

Into the same pan, boil enough water over high flame. Cook green beans for about 4 minutes or until softened and turns dark green. Drain into a colander and immediately transfer into a bowl of icy water.

Into a bowl, combine vinegar, mustard, and some salt to taste. Mix well to blend. Sprinkle black pepper to taste. Slowly whisk in oil until smoothly emulsified.

Evenly divide arugula onto 6 plates. Place potatoes and green beans on top of each other; season with salt and pepper to taste; then scatter roasted chestnuts all over the tops.

Sides 2

Oven-roasted Squash with Thyme

Makes: 4 servings
Total Time: 1 hour

- 12 oz. summer squash, quartered, seeded, cubed
- 1 1/2 cups fennel bulb, sliced
- 1 tbsp. fennel fronds, chopped, divided
- 1 tbsp. virgin olive oil
- 1 tbsp. fresh thyme, chopped
- 1/4 tsp. sea salt
- 1/4 tsp. freshly ground pepper
- 1/4 cup garlic, thinly sliced

Preheat oven to 450°F.
Into a bowl, mix cubed squash with sliced fennel, oil, and thyme, sprinkle salt and pepper to taste.

Evenly spread vegetable mixture on rimmed baking sheet and roast for about 10 minutes. Stir in garlic and roast for additional 5 minutes or until the squash is tender and fennel is starting to turn brown.

Serve with chopped fennel fronds.

Snacks

Alfalfa Sprout and Avocado in White Bread Sandwich

Makes 4 servings
Total time: 15 minutes

- 12 slices white sandwich bread
- 2 ripe avocados, pitted, diced
- 1 tsp. salt
- 1/4 tsp. freshly ground black pepper
- 1 bunch radishes, very thinly sliced
- 2 oz. alfalfa sprouts
- 8 oz. goat cheese, room temperature

Toast sandwich bread until lightly golden on both sides.

Into a bowl, mash avocados using the back side of a wooden spoon. Season with salt and pepper to taste. Spread mashed avocado on 8 toasted sandwiches. Layer radishes, alfalfa sprouts and crumbled cheese on tops. Stack and form 4 club sandwiches, each with 3 slices of toasted bread, 2 layers of avocado, radishes, alfalfa sprouts, and goat cheese. Slice in half diagonally and serve immediately.

Breakfast

Pain Perdu with Poached Eggs and Greens

Total Time: 45 minutes
Makes 2 Servings

- 6 slices baguette, diagonally cut 1-inch thick
- 1 cup whole milk
- 1 whole egg, beaten
- 2 large eggs, poached
- 1 tbsp. coconut butter, softened
- 1/2 cup cottage cheese, grated
- 2 tsp. apple cider vinegar
- 3 cups baby spinach
- 1 tbsp. virgin olive oil

Preheat oven to 400°F. Lightly grease a 9 inch pie dish and mat bottom with bread slices.

Into a bowl, whisk egg with salt and pepper to taste.

Pour all over the bread. Sprinkle cheese, pat lightly and set aside to soak for about 20 minutes.

Dot butter on the top and bake uncovered for about 23 minutes or until golden brown.

Meanwhile, into a deep saucepan, boil 2 inch water with some vinegar. Poach eggs for about 3 minutes or until desired doneness is reached.

Into a bowl, combine greens with remaining vinegar and oil. Season it with salt to taste. Plate bread slices into 2 separate plates and top with greens and poached eggs. Sprinkle some salt and pepper to taste.

Lunch

Okra and Tomatoes over Rice

Makes 6 servings
Total Time: 1 hour

- 2 tbsp. coconut oil
- 1 clove garlic, minced
- 1/2 onion, chopped
- 1/2 cup vegetable broth
- 1 1/2 lbs. okra, trimmed, cut into 1/2-inch pieces
- 4 plum tomatoes, chopped
- 2 sprigs fresh thyme
- 2 dried bay leaves
- Salt and freshly ground black pepper
- 3 cups steamed wild rice

Into a large pan, heat oil over medium flame until shimmering. Cook garlic and onions for about 3 minutes or until browned and translucent, respectively. Pour in vegetable broth, and cook with stirring until volume is reduced by half.

Mix in okra, tomatoes, bay leaves and thyme. Put cover and bring to simmer over lower flame; cook and stir for another 15 minutes or until okra is fork tender. Serve warm over steaming rice.

Dinner

Quinoa Stuffed Tomatoes with Goat Cheese

Total time: 47 minutes
Makes 4 servings

- ¼ cup quinoa, rinsed
- $1/3$ cup vegetable broth
- 4 large sized tomatoes
- ¼ tsp. sea salt
- ⅛ tsp. black pepper
- 3 tbsp. goat cheese, grated
- 2 tbsp. fresh basil, finely chopped
- 2 tbsp. fresh parsley, chopped
- 2 tsp. extra virgin olive oil

Preheat oven to 400 °F.

Into a saucepan, mix quinoa with vegetable broth and boil over medium high flame. Stir and simmer covered, over lower flame for about 15 minutes or until most of the liquid is absorb and quinoa has become fluffy.

While quinoa is cooking, prepare the tomatoes. Cut the tops of the tomatoes, removing the stem and chopping the remaining tops. Scoop out and discard the pulp and seeds and arrange them in an 8 inch square baking dish. Sprinkle salt and pepper to taste.

Into a bowl, combine chopped tomatoes with the cheese, parsley, basil, oil and the cooked quinoa. Mix to blend. Stuff the tomatoes and bake for about 12 minutes or until fully heated through and tomato skins are slightly creased.

Drinks

Fruits with Spinach and Parsley Carrot Juice

Makes 1 (1-cup) serving
Total time 10 minutes

- 1 cup pear, unpeeled, cut into large chunks
- 1 cup fresh pineapple, peeled, cored, cut into large chunks
- 1/2 medium carrot, peeled

- 2 cups spinach with stems
- 1 bunch fresh flat-leaf parsley with stems
- 1/4 cup freshly squeezed grapefruit juice

Into a heavy duty juicer, process pear, pineapple, spinach, parsley, and carrot. Skim out any generated foam. Mix in grapefruit juice, add ice cubes if desired, and serve. For best results, chill the ingredients first before processing.

Sides 1

Celery Root Mash with Goat's Milk

Makes 6 servings
Total time: 45 minutes

- 2 lbs. celery root, peeled, cubed
- 1/2 cup fresh goat's milk
- 3 tbsp. coconut oil
- Sea salt to taste
- celery root leaves, chopped for garnish

Into a pot, place 2 quarts water and 1 tbsp. salt and bring to a boil over high flame. Cook celery root for about 28 minutes or until fork tender. Drain into a colander and return to the pot. Heat on low, with occasional shaking for about a minute.

Pour in goat's milk, coconut oil and some salt to taste. Process with a potato masher until desired consistency is attained. Add more salt and pepper if desired.

Serve garnished with celery root leaves.

Sides 2

Baked Sweet Potato topped with Macadamia Nuts

Makes 2 servings
Total time: 1 hour 15 minutes

- 1/4 cup macadamia nuts
- 3 cups sweet potatoes, peeled, cut into wedges
- 1/4 cup virgin olive oil, divided

- Sea salt and ground pepper to taste
- 1/2 tbsp. balsamic vinegar
- 2 tsp. maple syrup
- 1/2 tsp. cinnamon powder

Preheat oven to 350°F.

Spread macadamia nuts on a baking dish and roast in the oven for about 7 minutes or until lightly browned. Cool and chop.

Raise oven temperature to 400°F. Lightly grease a baking dish.
Spread sweet potatoes on prepared dish, add 1 tbsp. of oil and toss to coat. Season with salt and pepper and bake for about an hour, stirring occasionally, until tender. Cool for a few minutes. Transfer to a serving platter.

Into a bowl, mix remaining oil with vinegar, maple syrup and cinnamon. Drizzle over sweet potatoes and top with roasted macadamia nuts.

Snacks

Vegetable Club Sandwich with Hummus

Makes 4 servings
Total time: 15 minutes

- 1 (15 1/2-oz.) can chickpeas, drained
- 1 tbsp. tahini
- 3 tbsp. plain fat-free yogurt
- 1 tbsp. lemon juice
- 1/2 tsp. ground cumin
- 2 garlic cloves, peeled
- 2 tbsp. water
- 1/4 tsp. salt
- 8 slices whole grain bread
- 1 red capsicum, sliced
- 1/2 cup baby arugula
- 2 plum tomatoes, sliced
- 1/3 cup clover or broccoli sprouts
- 4 radishes, thinly sliced
- 1 tbsp. roasted garlic-flavoured olive oil

- 1 tbsp. fresh lemon juice
- Salt and black pepper to taste

Into a food processor, combine the chickpeas, tahini, yogurt, lemon juice, cumin, garlic, water and salt. Process until smoothly pureed.

Lay 4 bread slices on a flat surface. On each, layer a spread of hummus, slices of bell peppers, tomatoes, arugula, radishes and sprouts. Into a bowl, whisk oil with lemon juice; season with salt and pepper to taste. Drizzle all over the vegetables.

Top each with a slice of bread and serve with a green juice.

Breakfast

Broiled Beans with Eggs and Herbs

Total Time: 35 minutes
Makes 4 servings

- 1 tsp. olive oil
- 2 small hot chilli peppers, diced
- 1 medium sweet potato, peeled, diced
- 1 medium onion, chopped
- 2 garlic cloves, chopped
- 2 medium tomatoes, diced
- 2 cups canned black beans, drained and rinsed well
- 1 tsp. smoked paprika
- 1 tsp. ground cumin
- 1 tsp. chilli powder
- 4 large eggs
- 4 tbsp. finely chopped cilantro leaves

- 1 oz. cottage cheese, crumbled
- 2 oz. avocados, thinly sliced

Preheat oven to 450 °F. Lightly grease 4 (16-oz.) ramekins.

Into a large skillet, heat oil over medium high flame and sauté pepper, garlic, onion, and potato for about 5 minutes. Mix in tomatoes, cumin, chilli powder paprika, and beans; cook covered for about 20 minutes, or until potatoes are tender.

Place about a cup of the vegetable mixture into prepared ramekins, spreading up to the edges, forming a hollow space in the centre. Place a cracked egg into each ramekins and abke for about 5 minutes or until eggs are just set. Remove ramekins from the oven while increasing its temperature to broil.

Broil for another 5 minutes or until eggs are well set. Serve warm with cilantro, cheese and avocado slices on tops.

Lunch

Garlicky Chicken with Mashed Potatoes

Makes 4 servings
Total Time: 25 minutes

- 3 lbs. chicken breast, quartered
- salt and freshly ground black pepper
- 2 tbsp. virgin olive oil
- 1 tbsp. coconut oil
- about 40 large garlic cloves, peeled, semi-crushed
- 1 cup vegetable broth
- 4 cups mashed potatoes

Into a bowl, sprinkle chicken with salt and pepper to taste.

Into a heavy non-stick pan, heat oils over medium high flame until shimmering. Cook chicken, skin side down for about 5 minutes or until it turns golden brown. Fry other sides for another 5 minutes. Work in batches.

Drain on paper towels.

Into the same pan and oil, stir in garlic cloves for about 3 minutes. Place back all the chicken and sauté for another 5 minutes or until garlic turns golden brown but not too scorched. Pour in vegetable stock, scraping pan's bottom.

Put cover and cook for another 15 minutes or until juice from meat runs clear and pan liquid has mostly evaporated and slightly thickened.

Serve immediately with mashed potatoes.

Dinner

Roasted Sweet Potato with Green Beans

Makes 6 servings
Total time: 45 minutes

- 2 large sweet potatoes, peeled, sliced lengthwise
- 1 cup Stevia

- 1 tsp. lemon juice
- 1/2 cup apple cider vinegar
- 3 tbsp. coconut oil, unsalted
- 1 tbsp. onions, diced
- 2 tbsp. white sugar
- 1/2 tsp. ground cloves
- 3/4 tsp. white pepper
- 1 pinch thyme
- 16 oz. package green beans whole, frozen
- 1/2 cup apple cider vinegar

Preheat oven to 400 °F.

Into a 9 x 13 inch baking dish, combine sweet potatoes with 1 cup stevia, lemon juice, and 1/2 cup apple cider vinegar. Mix well to blend and bake in oven for about 25 minutes, basting occasionally.

Meanwhile, heat oil into a pan over medium heat. Cook onions, thyme, cloves, white pepper and sugar. Add in green beans and sauté for about 2 minutes. Pour in remaining apple cider vinegar and continue cooking for another 2 minutes or until beans is tender. Set aside to keep warm.

Separate sweet potatoes from the pan juices and mix with the green beans. Serve warm with a little meat.

Drinks

Mango-Kale Juice

Makes 2 serving (16 ounces)
Total time 10 minutes

- 2 bunches kale
- 2 mangoes, pitted
- 1 large apple, sliced

Juice all of the ingredients in a juicer. Can last a day if chilled in an airtight glass container

Sides 1

Root Vegetable Slaw

Makes 4 servings
Total time: 25 minutes

- 1 tsp. Dijon mustard
- 1 tsp. sea salt
- 1 tsp. white sugar
- 1/4 cup red wine vinegar
- 1 cup parsley, chopped
- 2/3 cup olive oil
- 1 small celery root, peeled, shredded
- 2 black radishes, shredded
- 2 large carrots, peeled, shredded
- 2 medium parsnips, peeled, shredded

Into a large blender, combine vinegar, parsley mustard, salt, and sugar. Blend for about 30 seconds until well mixed. Scrape sides and run at lowest speed. Gradually pour in oil and then turn to highest speed and blend for about 90 seconds.

Into a salad bowl, combine all shreeded vegetables, pour in pureed dressing and toss to fully coat. Cover with plastic wrap and chill for at least 20 minutes.

Sides 2

Stir-fried Asparagus with Curry

Makes: 4 servings
Total Time: 40 minutes

- 2 tsp. coconut oil, melted
- 1 tsp. curry powder
- 1/2 tsp. lemon juice
- sea salt to taste
- 2 tsp. virgin olive oil
- 1 shallot, finely diced
- 1 lb. asparagus, trimmed and cut into 1-inch spears

Into a bowl, whisk coconut oil with lemon juice, curry powder and some salt to taste.

Into a pan, heat olive oil over medium flame. Sauté shallots for about 2 minutes or until tender. Add asparagus; cook and stir for about 4 minutes or until tender. Put off heat, mix in the curry mixture and toss to blend.

Snacks

Orange Chia Seeds Pudding

Makes 4 servings
Total time: overnight

- 2 oranges, peeled, segmented, white pith removed
- ½ tsp. orange zest
- 1 cup whole milk
- 1/4 cup chia seeds
- 3 tbsp. maple syrup
- 1/8 tsp. grated nutmeg

Into a container fitted with airtight cap, combine orange zest, milk, chia, maple syrup, and nutmeg. Cover, shake, and chill for about 10 hours or until thick. Peel and segment oranges and chill for the same time.

Transfer pudding into individual serving bowls or wide-mouth glasses and top each with oranges.

Breakfast

Artichoke Frittata

Makes 2 servings
Total Time: 35 minutes

- 2 tsp. extra-virgin olive oil, divided
- 2 cloves garlic, minced
- 1 medium red bell pepper, diced
- 1/4 tsp. crushed red pepper
- 4 large eggs
- 1 (14 oz.) can artichoke hearts, rinsed and coarsely chopped
- 1/4 cup cottage cheese, freshly grated
- 1 tsp. dried oregano
- 1/4 tsp. salt, or to taste
- Freshly ground pepper, to taste

Into a pan with heat resistant handles, heat 1 tbsp. oil over medium heat. Cook bell peppers for about 2 minutes or until tender. Mix in red peppers and garlic and cook for another 2 minutes. Slide into a plate and wipe clean the pan.

Into a bowl, beat eggs until smooth. Add artichoke hearts, oregano, cheese salt, and sautéed bell pepper mixture.

Preheat oven to its broiling temperature.

Into the same pan, heat remaining oil over medium heat. Spread egg mixture into the pan, cook for about 3 minutes, lifting sides using spatula to allow uncooked egg to flow underneath. Broil the egg for about 2 minutes.

Serve frittata sliced into wedges.

Lunch

Five-Veggie Stir-Fry

Makes 4 servings

Total time: 50 minutes

- 1 cup white rice, rinsed
- 1 cup vegetable broth
- 2 tbsp. arrowroot powder
- 1/2 tsp. ground ginger
- 1 cup orange juice
- 1/4 cup reduced-sodium soy sauce
- 1 tbsp. vegetable broth
- 2 cloves garlic, minced
- 1 tbsp. olive oil
- 1 cup cubed firm tofu
- 2 large carrots, sliced
- 2 cups broccoli florets
- 2 cups cauliflower florets
- 1 tsp. olive oil
- 1 cup fresh mushrooms, quartered
- 1 cup fresh snow peas
- 1 egg, lightly beaten
- 1/4 cup slivered almonds

Into a saucepan, combine rinsed rice with the vegetable broth. Bring to a boil over medium high heat. Lower heat, cover and simmer for about 25 minutes or until almost all liquid have been absorbed and rice tender.

Into a small bowl, dissolve arrowroot powder in orange juice. Mix in ginger, soy sauce and broth.

Into a large pan, heat oil over medium-high heat and cook broccoli, carrots, and cauliflower for about 4 minutes or until just tender. Mix in oil, tofu, snow peas, and mushrooms; cook and stir for another 3 minutes or until all are tender.

Push aside vegetables, creating a clear centre where egg will be cooked until set. Mix egg with the rest in the pan. Pour in orange juice mixture and bring to a boil; cook for about 2 minutes or until thickened.

Scoop a mound of cooked rice on 4 plates. Top this with the vegetables and slivered almonds.

Dinner

Zucchini Spaghetti with fresh Tomato Sauce.

Makes 1 serving
Total time: 15 minutes

- 2 zucchinis, peeled, seeded, grated
- 1 tbsp. olive oil
- 1/4 cup water
- salt and ground black pepper to taste
- 4 plum tomatoes, chopped
- 1/4 cup olive oil
- 3 cloves garlic, minced
- fresh basil, chopped

Into a pan, heat olive oil over medium flame; and cook and stir zucchini for about a minute. Add water and cook for another 6 minutes or until zucchini is tender. Season with salt and pepper. Transfer into a bowl. Wipe clean the pan.

Into the same pan, heat ¼ cup olive oil over medium

flame. Cook garlic for about 3 minutes or until aromatic. Mix in chopped tomatoes, cook and stir for another 5 minutes or until saucy.

Pour sauce over the zucchini, toss to coat. Sprinkle basil leaves on top and enjoy.

Drinks

Apple, Beet and Carrot Juice

Makes 4 to 6 servings
Total time 10 minutes

- 6 medium beets, trimmed, peeled
- 4 large carrots, trimmed, peeled
- 2 apples cored, halved
- 1 (3" piece) fresh ginger, peeled
- 3 tbsp. fresh lemon juice

Juice beets, apples, carrots and ginger through a juicer machine. Discard solids. Stir in lemon juice. Serve at once in glasses.

Sides 1

Seaweed Tempura

Makes 6 servings

- 1 cup seaweed, washed, thinly sliced lengthwise
- 1/3 cup plus 3 tbsp. almond flour
- Sea salt
- 2 tbsp. sesame seeds
- 5 oz. soda water
- canola oil, for frying
- Soy sauce, low sodium

Into a bowl, combine together flour, sesame seeds and salt to taste. Mix well. Slowly pour in soda water, whisking continuously until blended.

Into a deep pan, heat about 2 inches oil over medium heat. Coat seaweed slices with the batter and fry by batches into the hot oil until lightly browned. Stir to untangle strands.

Use slotted spoon to remove and transfer fried seaweed on a paper-lined plates to drain excess oil.

Season with some salt and pepper to taste. Serve warm with low sodium soy sauce as dip.

Sides 2

Steamed Green Beans with Rice Wine Vinegar Vinaigrette

Makes 9 servings
Total time: 20 minutes

- 1 1/2 lbs. fresh green beans, trimmed
- 1/3 cup sweet red pepper, diced
- 4 tsp. olive oil
- 4 tsp. water
- 1 tsp. rice wine vinegar
- 1 tsp. spicy brown mustard
- 3/4 tsp. sea salt
- 1/4 tsp. black pepper
- 1/8 tsp. garlic powder

Into a steamer, cook greens beans along with bell peppers for about 8 minutes or until crisp and tender.

While the beans are cooking, prepare the dressing. Into a bowl whisk vinegar, water, oil, mustard, garlic powder, salt and pepper until well blended.

Into a bowl, combine steamed vegetable with the dressing. Toss to blend.

Snacks

Carrot and Celery Sticks with Avocado Dip

Makes 4 servings
Total time:

- 5 carrots, scrubbed, sliced into pears
- 5 stalks celery, washed sliced into pears
- 1 yellow bell pepper, seeded, sliced lengthwise

  Avocado Dip
- 3 medium avocados, peeled, pitted

- 1 tbsp. lemon juice
- ½ tsp. sea salt
- ½ tsp. chilli powder
- ¼ tsp. cumin

Into a bowl, crush avocados using back part of a wooden spoon until chunky mashed. Mix in lemon juice, cumin and chilli powder. Season with salt and pepper to taste. Mix to blend.

Serve carrot and celery sticks with the avocado dip.

Breakfast

Healthy Cereal

Prep Time: 1 minute
Cook Time: 5 minutes

Ingredients

- 1/3 cup unsweetened coconut flakes
- 2 tbsp. chia seeds
- 2 tbsp. almonds, sliced
- 2 tbsp. hemp seeds
- 1 oz. wild blueberries
- 1 cup almond milk
- Stevia to taste

Into a bowl, combine all ingredients and mix. Set aside chilled for about 10 minutes and enjoy.

Lunch

Baked Mushrooms and Potatoes with Spinach

Makes 4 servings
Total time: 45 minutes

- 1 lb. potatoes, washed, halved
- 2 tbsp. olive oil
- 1/2 lb. Portobello mushrooms
- 6 cloves unpeeled garlic, crushed
- 2 tbsp. fresh thyme, chopped
- 1 tbsp. olive oil
- sea salt and ground black pepper to taste
- 1/4 lb. cherry tomatoes
- 2 tbsp. toasted pine nuts
- 1/4 lb. spinach, thinly sliced

Preheat oven to 425 °F.

Into a roasting pan, spread potatoes, drizzle 2 tbsp. oil and roast for about 15 minutes, turning sides once. Add Portobello mushrooms, head side down, and garlic cloves; season with salt and pepper and roast for 5 minutes more.

Add cherry tomatoes into the pan and roast for another 5 minutes. Evenly divide potatoes, mushroom and tomatoes on 4 plates. Scatter pine nuts and serve with sliced spinach.

Dinner

Stir-fried Kale and Mushroom

Makes 4 servings
Total time: 30 minutes

- 1 tsp. macadamia oil
- 1 onion, diced
- 1/2 cup shiitake mushrooms, sliced
- 3 cloves garlic, minced
- 1 tbsp. butter
- 1 tbsp. balsamic vinegar
- 1 pinch salt and ground black pepper to taste

- 1 bunch kale leaves, torn
- 1/2 cup vegetable stock.
- 1/2 tsp. nutmeg, freshly grated
- strips of cooked chicken

Into a large skillet, heat oil over medium high flame. Sauté onions, garlic and mushrooms for about 5 minutes or until mushrooms are softened. Mix in butter and balsamic vinegar then season with salt and pepper to taste. Cook and stir for another minute until well cooked.

Remove from heat and add kale. Slowly mix and cook with residual heat for about 5 minutes or until kale turns bright green and wilted. Sprinkle nutmeg, toss and serve with strips of cooked chicken.

Drinks

Cucumber, Celery and Orange Juice

Makes 6 servings
Total time 10 minutes

- 2 lbs. medium cucumbers, trimmed, seeded
- 1 bunch of celery with ribs
- 2 fresh oranges, peeled, seeded
- 1 1/2 tsp. honey

Into a juicer, process cucumber, celery and oranges. Mix in honey, add some ice cubes and enjoy.

Sides1

Mashed Split Green Peas

Makes 4 servings
Total time: 15 minutes

- 1 lb. cooked split green peas, frozen
- 2 tbsp. unsalted butter, divided
- 1/4 cup water
- 1 tbsp. lemon juice
- sea salt and cracked black pepper
- 1 tbsp. mint, finely chopped

Into a small pan, combined frozen peas with half of

butter and some water. Heat over medium flame for about 15 minutes or until peas are totally thawed and butter is melted. Put off flame and mashed using a potato masher or back of wood spoon until desired consistency is achieved.

Drizzle lemon juice, and add remaining half of the butter. Season with salt and pepper to taste. Mix to blend. Serve garnished with mint.

Sides 2

Mashed Potato with Bananas

Makes 4 servings
Total time: 1 hour

- 4 medium potatoes, scrubbed
- 2 ripe bananas
- 1 tsp. cinnamon
- 1/2 tsp. nutmeg
- Sea salt and pepper to taste
- 2 tbsp. butter
- 2 tbsp. maple syrup

Preheat oven to 400 °F.

Pierce holes in both potatoes and bananas. Place sweet potatoes on a baking sheet and bake for about 45 minutes, join the bananas in the oven 15 minutes before set time.

Peel sweet potatoes and bananas and mash in a bowl.

Into a pan, heat butter over medium flame. Fry patty-size portions of the mashed mixture, for about 3 minutes per side or until edges turn brown and crisp.

Top with maple syrup.

Snacks

Oven Fried Eggplant

Total Time: 35 minutes
Makes 4 Servings

- 1/2 cup fat-free mayonnaise

- 1 tbsp. onion, minced
- 1 lb. unpeeled eggplant, thickly sliced
- 1/3 cup fine bread crumbs
- 1/3 cup cottage cheese, grated
- 1/2 tsp. dried Italian seasoning
- coconut oil for greasing

Into a bowl, whisk mayonnaise with minced onion. Coat all side of eggplant slices with the mixture.

Into another bowl, mix cottage cheese, breadcrumbs, and Italian seasoning; dredge eggplant in this mixture and arrange, in single layer, on a lightly greased baking sheet.

Bake in a preheated 425 °F oven for about 24 minutes turning sides once at the middle of the set time.

Breakfast

Quinoa and Sweet Potato Skillet

Makes 4 servings
Total time:

- 1 small sweet potato, diced
- 3 tbsp. coconut oil
- 1/2 red onion, chopped
- 1/2 green pepper, chopped
- 1/2 red pepper, chopped
- 2 garlic cloves, minced
- 1 cup sliced mushrooms, chopped
- 1/2 cup uncooked quinoa, rinsed
- 1 cup low-sodium vegetable stock
- 4 eggs, poached
- salt and pepper to taste

Into a pan, heat oil over medium flame and cook sweet potatoes, mushrooms, onions, peppers, and garlic, covered for about 5 minutes with stirring until tender.

Mix in quinoa; cook and stir for about 2 minutes until quinoa is lightly browned. Pour in vegetable stock and boil. Lower flame at once and simmer covered for about 15 minutes.

Transfer quinoa-potato mixture into 4 serving bowls, season with salt and pepper to taste. Serve with poach eggs on tops.

Lunch

Carrot-Bean Sprouts Salad

Makes 4 servings
Total time: 12 minutes

- 1/2 cup bean sprouts
- 2 cups carrots, grated
- 1 tbsp. lemon juice
- 1 tsp. white sugar
- 1 tbsp. fresh coconut, grated

- 1 tbsp. cilantro, finely chopped
- 1 tbsp. sunflower seed oil
- 1 tsp. mustard seed
- salt to taste
- cuts of roasted turkey

Into a large salad bowl, combine carrots, bean sprouts, coconut, and cilantro. Into a small bowl, whisk sugar with lemon juice and drizzle all over the salad. Toss to fully coat.

Into a pan, heat oil over medium flame. Toast mustard seed until golden brown. Scatter all over the salad along with the frying sunflower seed oil. Season with salt and serve with some roasted turkey.

Dinner

Kumquat and Baby Greens Salad

Makes 4 servings
Total Time: 20 minutes

- 1/3 cup virgin olive oil
- 1/3 cup rice vinegar
- 1 tsp. brown sugar
- 1/4 tsp. black pepper, freshly ground
- 5 oz. mixed baby greens
- 2 green onions, chopped
- 1/2 cup celery, chopped
- 1 carrot, julienned
- 1/2 cup broccoli florets
- 1/2 cup cauliflower florets
- 1 avocado, peeled, pitted and diced
- 1 tsp. fresh lemon juice
- 2 oz. goat cheese, grated
- 3 oz. pine nuts, toasted
- 4 oz. kumquats - rinsed, seeded and sliced

Into a small jar fitted with a lid, combine virgin olive oil, rice vinegar, brown sugar, and pepper. Shake well to fully blend.

Into a large salad bowl, combine baby salad greens, cauliflower carrot, broccoli, green onions, celery and avocado. Drizzle with lemon juice, and toss to blend.

Scatter cheese, kumquats and pine nuts. Drizzle olive oil dressing and toss to mix well. Serve with any favourite slices of meat.

Drinks

Cucumber, Parsley and Tomato Juice

Makes 1 serving
Total time 10 minutes

- 1 handful of parsley
- 2 tomatoes
- 1/2 cucumber
- 2 celery stalks
- 1/8 onion

Juice the parsley first, then the rest of the ingredients, pour into a glass, drink and be delighted with its effect.

Sides 1

Tofu with Capsicum and Almonds

Makes 4 serving
Total time: 15 minutes

- 3 tbsp. olive oil
- 2 large red bell peppers, seeded, thinly sliced
- 3 large garlic cloves, finely chopped
- 3 tbsp. fresh ginger, peeled, minced
- 15 oz. extra-firm tofu, drained well, cubed
- 3 green onions, thinly sliced on diagonal
- 3 tbsp. low sodium soy sauce
- 2 tbsp. fresh lime juice
- 1/2 to 3/4 tsp. dried red pepper, crushed
- 6 oz. baby spinach leaves
- 1/3 cup fresh basil, chopped
- 1/3 cup lightly salted roasted almonds, chopped

Into a large pan, heat oil over medium high flame. Cook and stir ginger, garlic and bell peppers for about 2 minutes or until tender. Add in tofu cubes, toss for 2 minutes. Mix in onions, soy sauce and lime juice; cook for another minute. Add spinach in 3 batches, mixing after every addition and cook for a minute more until wilted. Add chopped basil leaves; then season with salt and pepper to taste.

Serve with toasted almonds on tops.

Sides 2

Creamy Mashed Cauliflower

Makes: 4 servings
Prep: 15 minutes
Total Time: 30 minutes

- 8 cups cauliflower, cut into florets
- 4 cloves garlic, crushed and peeled
- 1/3 cup whole milk
- 2 tsp. lemon juice
- 4 tsp. olive oil, divided
- 1 tsp. coconut oil
- 1/2 tsp. salt

- Freshly ground pepper, to taste
- fresh chives, chopped, for garnish

Into a steamer, cook cauliflower for about 13 minutes or until tender.

Into a food processor, combine steamed cauliflower with garlic along with milk, lemon juice, 2 tsp. olive oil, coconut oil, salt and pepper. Pulse then process until pureed.

Transfer into 4 serving bowls. Drizzle remaining 2 tsp. olive oil on tops and garnish with chopped chives. Serve warm.

Snacks

Watermelon Lime Salad

Makes 6 Servings
Total time: 10 minutes

- 1 lime, juiced, zested, chopped
- 1/4 cup white sugar
- 4 cups watermelon, cubed

Into a small saucepan, mix lime juice, lime zest and chopped parts; along with sugar and 1/4 cup water. Boil over high heat. Put off heat and set aside to cool.
Into a bowl, place watermelon cubes, Drizzle lime dressing, toss to blend. Serve immediately or chill for several minutes before serving.

Conclusion

This diet is anchored in the theory that acid-forming foods such as meats, and processed foods coupled with unhealthy lifestyle create an unhealthy environment for the body causing inflammations and an eventual disease. To offset this condition, a diet rich in vegetables and fruits which are alkaline-forming foods is necessary.

The pH of a body to be on prime condition should remain at about 7.4. Too much alkalinity is equally bad with too much acidity. The key to achieving neutral pH is proper food combinations. It is by having 80% of alkalizing foods and 20 % of acidifying foodstuffs. This ratio will also ensure the supply of equally important proteins, calcium and other essential nutrients acid-forming foods contain. Although such nutrition can also be sourced from specific alkaline-forming foods, if only one knows.

Medical Science offers no comprehensive studies yet to strongly back up this Alkaline Diet's claim. But many observational studies and centuries of culinary experience, proved that vegetables and fruits are far more better than meats and processed foods in supporting a healthy human body.

The theory goes that consuming acid-inducing foods and drinks creates an unhealthy cellular cnvironment and sends distress signals throughout the body, leading to colds, outbreaks, and inflammation. It's suggested this continual acid-dumping via food can create chronic disease such as arthritis, osteoporosis, and cancer. Proponents say you can think of it like a sliding scale—the more you eat and drink your way left, the more work your body must do to get back to normal. And making your body work really hard day in and day out will ultimately take its toll.

RECOMMENDED ALKALINE FOOD AND DIET BOOKS:

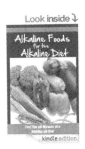

<u>Alkaline Foods For The Alkaline Diet: Feel The pH Miracle of a Healthy pH Diet</u>

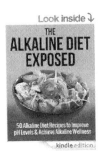

<u>The Alkaline Diet Exposed: 50 Alkaline Diet Recipes to Improve pH Levels and Achieve Alkaline Wellness</u>

BONUS: Free Books & Special Offers

I want to thank you again for purchasing this book! I would like to give you access to a great service that will e-mail you notifications when we have FREE books available. You will have FREE access to some great titles before they get marked at the normal retail price that everyone else will pay. This is a no strings attached offer simply for being a great customer.

*Simply go to: <u>www.globalizedhealing.com</u> to get access now.

42803712R00088

Made in the USA
Lexington, KY
06 July 2015